Contents

Centimetres and millimetres	3-5
Centimetres and metres	6
Metres, centimetres and millimetres	7-8
Volume	9-10
Area	11-15
Telling the time	16-18
Timing	19-21
24 hour clock	22-24
Horizontal and vertical	25
Parallel lines	26
Parallel and perpendicular lines	27
Naming shapes	28-29
Circles	30-32
Naming shapes	33-34
Line symmetry	35-37
Rotational symmetry	38-40
Tessellating	41-42
Degrees	43-45
Measuring angles	46-48
Coordinates	49-51
Bar-line graphs	52-54
Averages	55-57
Frequency tables	58-60
Listing outcomes	61-62
Throwing dice	63
Picking cubes	64

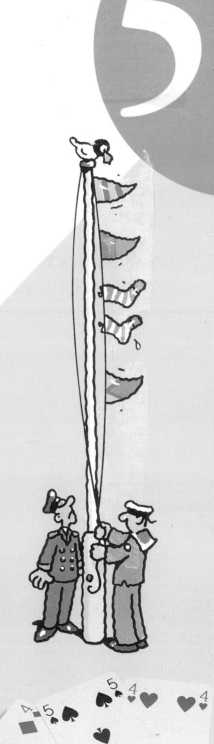

How to use this book

Each page has a title telling you what it is about.

Instructions look like this. Always read these carefully before starting.

Sometimes there is a 'Hint' to help you.

Sometimes you need materials to help you with the activity.

This shows you how to set out your work. The first question is usually done for you.

This shows that the activity is an 'Explore'. Work with a friend.

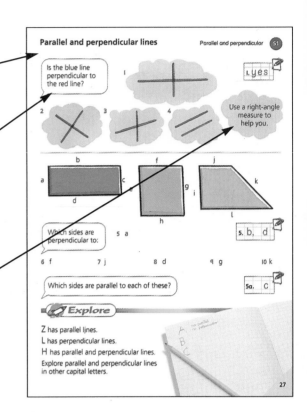

Centimetres and millimetres

Write each length in millimetres.

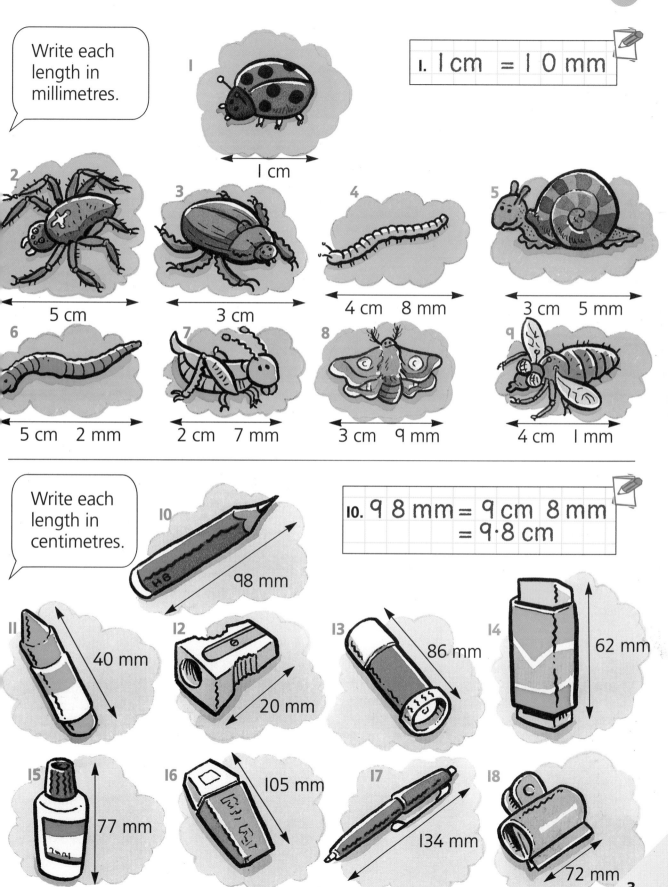

I. **1 cm = 1 0 mm**

1 cm

2 — 5 cm

3 — 3 cm

4 — 4 cm   8 mm

5 — 3 cm   5 mm

6 — 5 cm   2 mm

7 — 2 cm   7 mm

8 — 3 cm   9 mm

9 — 4 cm   1 mm

Write each length in centimetres.

10. **9 8 mm = 9 cm 8 mm**
    = 9·8 cm

10 — 98 mm

11 — 40 mm

12 — 20 mm

13 — 86 mm

14 — 62 mm

15 — 77 mm

16 — 105 mm

17 — 134 mm

18 — 72 mm

3

Centimetres and millimetres

Find one of each object.

Measure it in centimetres and millimetres.

1. 1 2 cm 6 mm

1

2

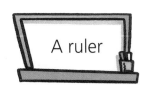

A ruler

3

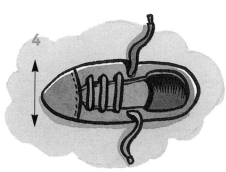

4

5

6

7

8

9

Cut strips of paper to match these lengths.

Stick them in your book.

Label each with its length.

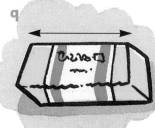

A ruler, scissors, paper

| 10 | 4 cm 4 mm | 11 | 5 cm 2 mm | 12 | 6 cm 3 mm |

| 13 | 7 cm 1 mm | 14 | 4 cm 9 mm | 15 | 3 cm 8 mm | 16 | 5 cm 7 mm |

Centimetres and millimetres

Measure each line.

Write the lengths in centimetres.

a. 3·2 cm

A ruler

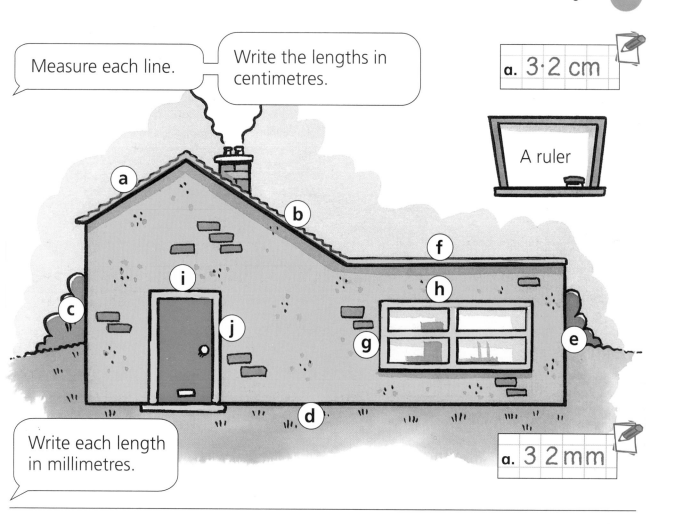

Write each length in millimetres.

a. 3 2 mm

Draw lines of these lengths.

l   3 cm 8 mm

l. 3 cm 8 mm

2   4 cm 2 mm   3   2 cm 9 mm   4   5 cm 5 mm   5   1 cm 3 mm

6   3 cm 4 mm   7   4 cm 1 mm   8   3 cm 2 mm   9   6 cm 4 mm

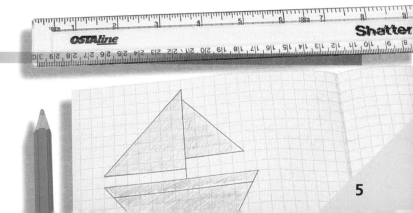

Explore

Draw a picture using only straight lines.

Label each line with its length.

Centimetres and metres

Write each height in centimetres.

I

1·6 m

1. $1·6 m = 160 cm$

2

1·7 m

3

1·3 m

4

1·1 m

5

1·2 m

6

1·8 m

7

$1\frac{1}{2}$ m

8

1·4 m

9

1·5 m

Write each length in metres and centimetres.

10. $217 cm = 2 m \ 17 cm$

10

217 cm

11

426 cm

12

130 cm

13

368 cm

14

284 cm

15

195 cm

Metres, centimetres and millimetres

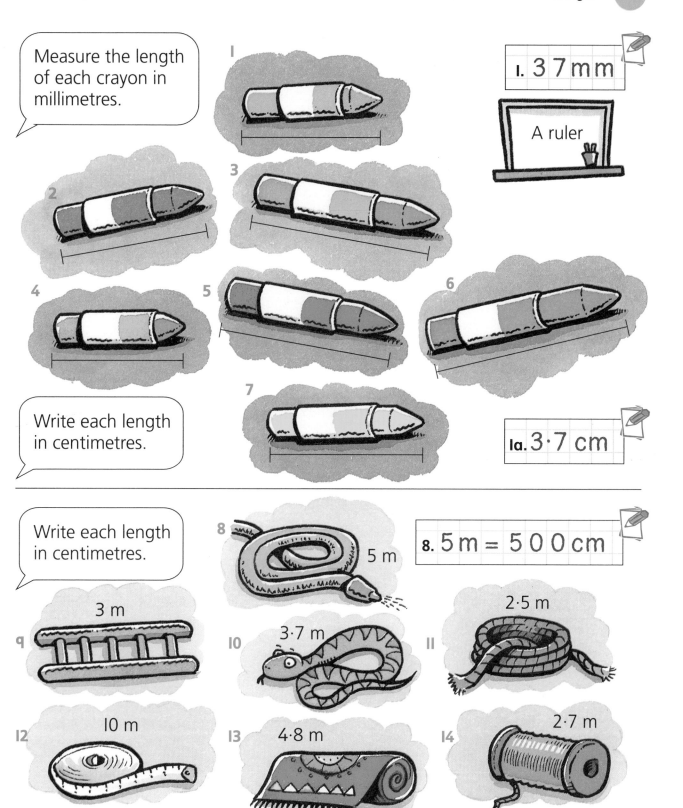

Measure the length of each crayon in millimetres.

1. 37 mm

A ruler

Write each length in centimetres.

1a. 3·7 cm

Write each length in centimetres.

8. 5 m = 500 cm

Write each length in millimetres.

8a. 5000 mm

7

Metres, centimetres and millimetres

Write the missing numbers.

1   m = 100 cm

1. 1 m = 1 0 0 cm

2 1 cm = mm

3 50 mm = cm

4   m = 1400 cm

5 20 cm = mm

6   mm = $\frac{1}{2}$ cm

7 200 cm = m

8 $\frac{1}{2}$ m = cm

9 100 mm = cm

10 12 m = cm

11   m = 1000 mm

12 10 m = cm

13   m = 2000 cm

14   cm = 20 mm

15 2 m = mm

16   m = 3000 cm

 **Explore**

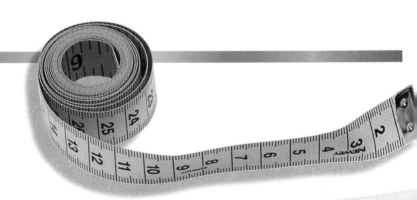

Measure 5 objects, each one at least 1 metre long.

Write each length in:
- a   metres
- b   centimetres
- c   millimetres.

table → 1·6 m

bookshelf → 1·2 m

Volume

Write the volume of each cuboid.

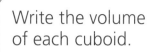

1

3 cm · 3 cm · 3 cm

1. $3 \times 3 = 9$

$3 \times 9 = 27 \, cm^3$

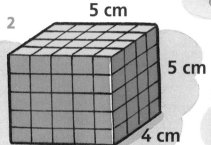

2 5 cm · 5 cm · 4 cm

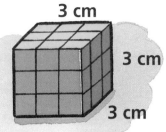

3 2 cm · 2 cm · 5 cm

Find how many cubes in a layer. How many layers?

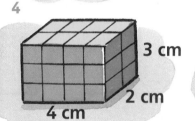

4 3 cm · 2 cm · 4 cm

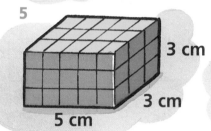

5 3 cm · 3 cm · 5 cm

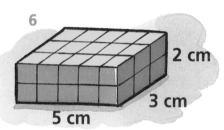

6 2 cm · 3 cm · 5 cm

Write the volume of each cuboid.

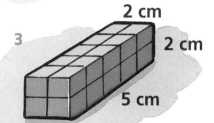

7 4 cm · 5 cm · 5 cm

7. $5 \times 5 = 25$

$4 \times 25 = 100 \, cm^3$

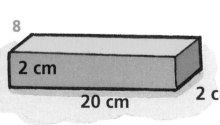

8 2 cm · 20 cm · 2 cm

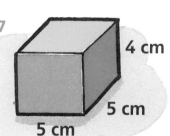

9 2 cm · 6 cm · 3 cm

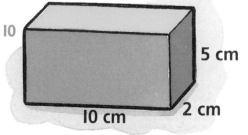

10 5 cm · 10 cm · 2 cm

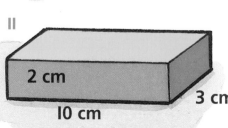

11 2 cm · 10 cm · 3 cm

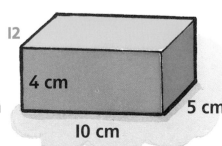

12 4 cm · 10 cm · 5 cm

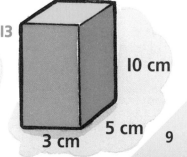

13 10 cm · 3 cm · 5 cm

9

Volume

Write the volume of each tank.

1. $10 \times 10 = 100$

$4 \times 100 = 400 \, cm^3$

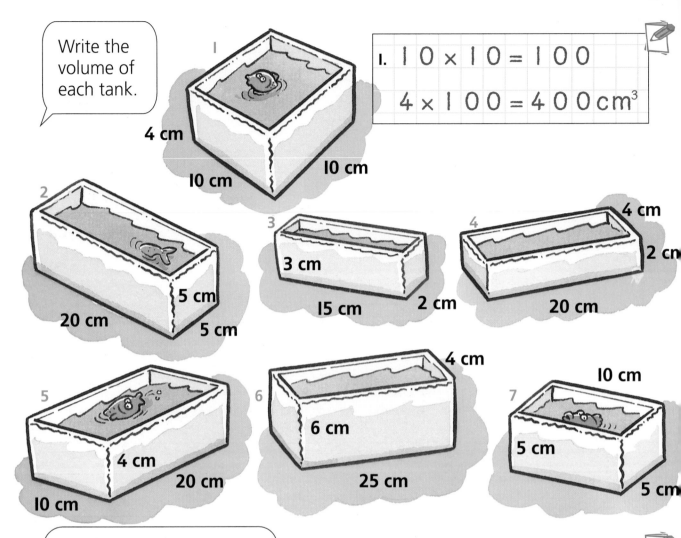

1   4 cm   10 cm

2   5 cm   20 cm   5 cm

3   3 cm   15 cm   2 cm

4   4 cm   2 cm   20 cm

5   4 cm   20 cm   10 cm

6   6 cm   25 cm   4 cm

7   10 cm   5 cm   5 cm

Write how many millilitres each tank can hold.

1a. $400 \, cm^3 = 400 \, ml$

Explore

This cuboid has a volume of 36 cm³.

How many other cuboids have this volume?

Write the length, width and height of each.

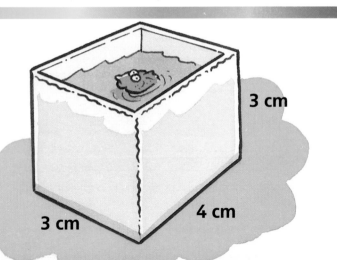

3 cm   3 cm   4 cm

Area

Write the area of each rectangle.

1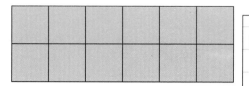

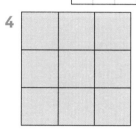
1. area = 2 × 6
   = 12 cm²

2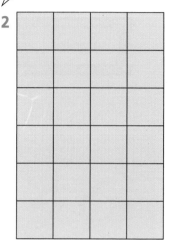

3

4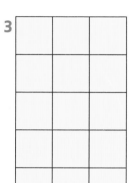

The squares are square centimetres.

5

7

6

Write the area of each rectangle.

The squares are square centimetres.

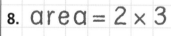
8. area = 2 × 3
   = 6 cm²

8

9

10

11

13

12

Area

> Measure the length and width of each sticker.

> Write the area.

1. length = 4 cm
   width = 3 cm
   area   = 12 cm^2

1

2

3

A ruler

4

5

6

7

> Measure the length and width of each rectangle.

> Write the area.

8. length = 8 cm
   width = 7 cm
   area   = 56 cm^2

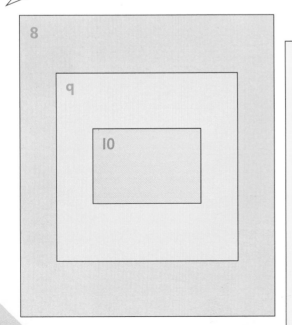
8
9
10

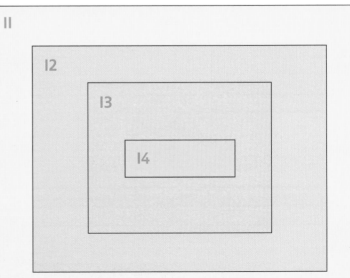
11
12
13
14

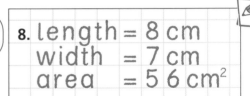

Area

Copy each shape.

Divide it into 2 rectangles.

Write the total area.

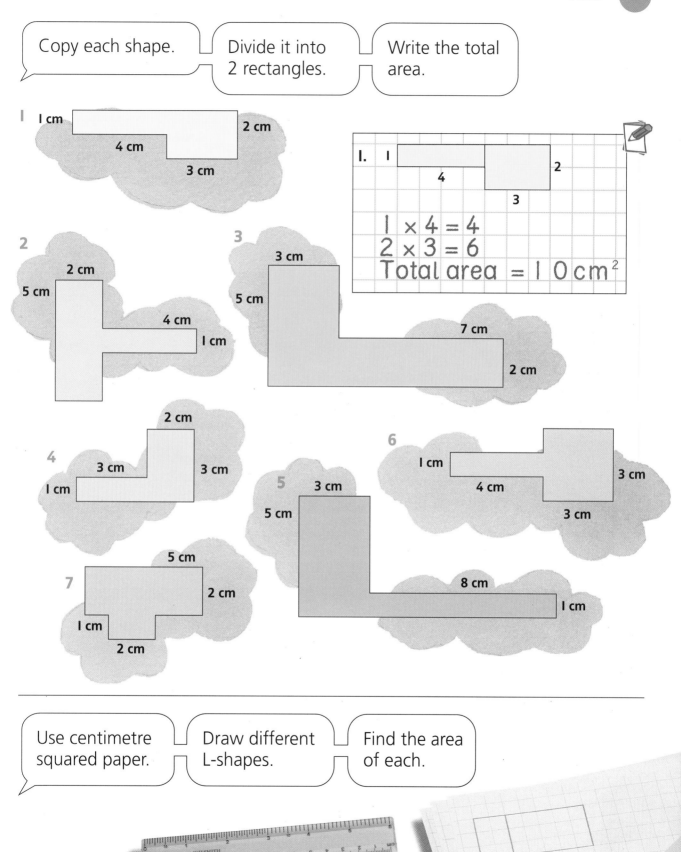

1. 1
   4
   2
   3

   $1 \times 4 = 4$
   $2 \times 3 = 6$
   Total area $= 10 \, cm^2$

1   1 cm   2 cm   4 cm   3 cm

2   2 cm   5 cm   4 cm   1 cm

3   3 cm   5 cm   7 cm   2 cm

4   2 cm   3 cm   3 cm   1 cm

5   3 cm   5 cm   8 cm   1 cm

6   1 cm   4 cm   3 cm   3 cm

7   5 cm   2 cm   1 cm   2 cm

Use centimetre squared paper.

Draw different L-shapes.

Find the area of each.

$6 \times 2 = 12$
$3 \times 5 = 15$
area = 27

13

Area

Write the area of each red triangle.

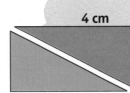

1
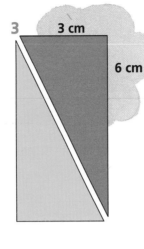
4 cm
2 cm

1. $2 \times 4 = 8$
$A = \frac{1}{2}$ of $8 = 4$ cm^2

2
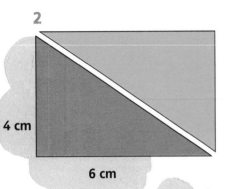
4 cm
6 cm

3
3 cm
6 cm

4
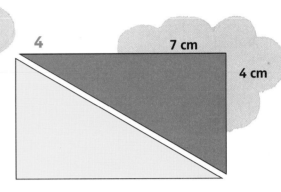
7 cm
4 cm

5
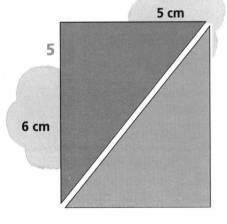
5 cm
6 cm

6
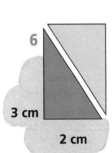
3 cm
2 cm

7
2 cm
5 cm

8
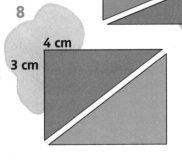
4 cm
3 cm

Write the area of each triangle.

9
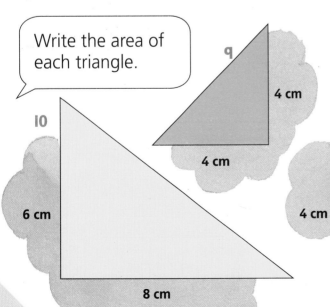
4 cm
4 cm

9. $4 \times 4 = 16$
$A = \frac{1}{2}$ of $16 = 8$ cm^2

10
6 cm
8 cm

11
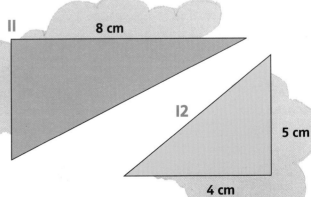
8 cm
4 cm

12
5 cm
4 cm

14

Area

Write the area of each flag.

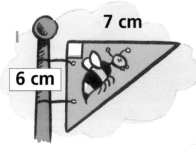
1 7 cm
6 cm

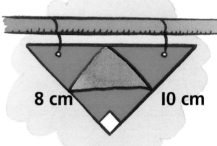
I. $6 \times 7 = 42$
$\frac{1}{2}$ of $42 = 21$ cm^2

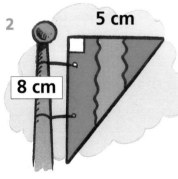
2 5 cm
8 cm

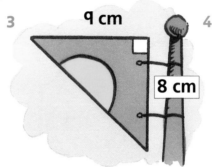
3 9 cm
8 cm

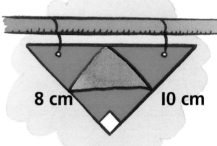
4
8 cm   10 cm

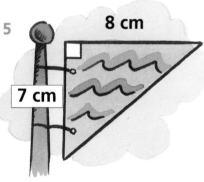
5 8 cm
7 cm

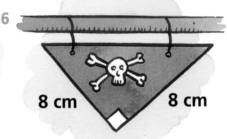
6
8 cm   8 cm

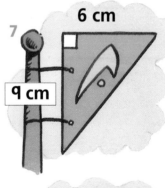
7 6 cm
9 cm

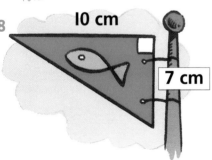
8 10 cm
7 cm

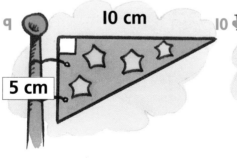
9 10 cm
5 cm

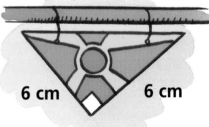
10
6 cm   6 cm

Explore

How many right-angled triangles can you draw with an area of 24 cm^2?

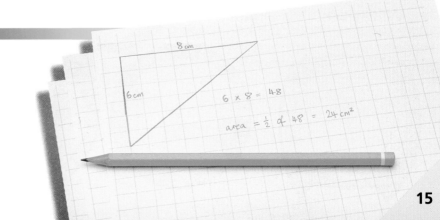

8 cm

6 cm

$6 \times 8 = 48$

area $= \frac{1}{2}$ of $48 = 24$ cm^2

15

Telling the time

Which clocks match?

1. a and h

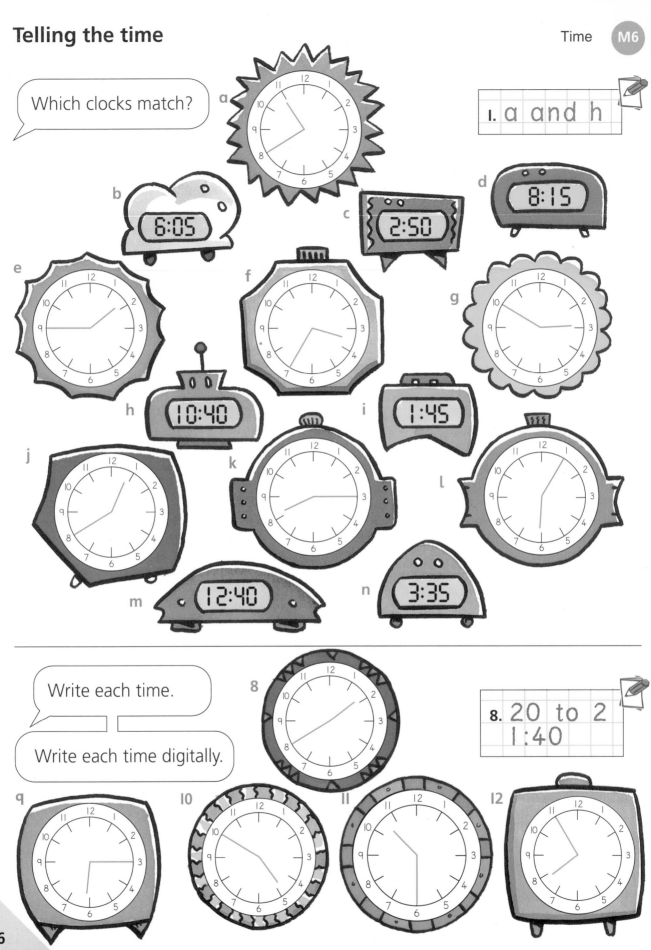

a

b 6:05

c 2:50

d 8:15

e

f

g

h 10:40

i 1:45

j

k

l

m 12:40

n 3:35

Write each time.

Write each time digitally.

8

8. 20 to 2
   1:40

9

10

11

12

16

Telling the time

Which clocks match?

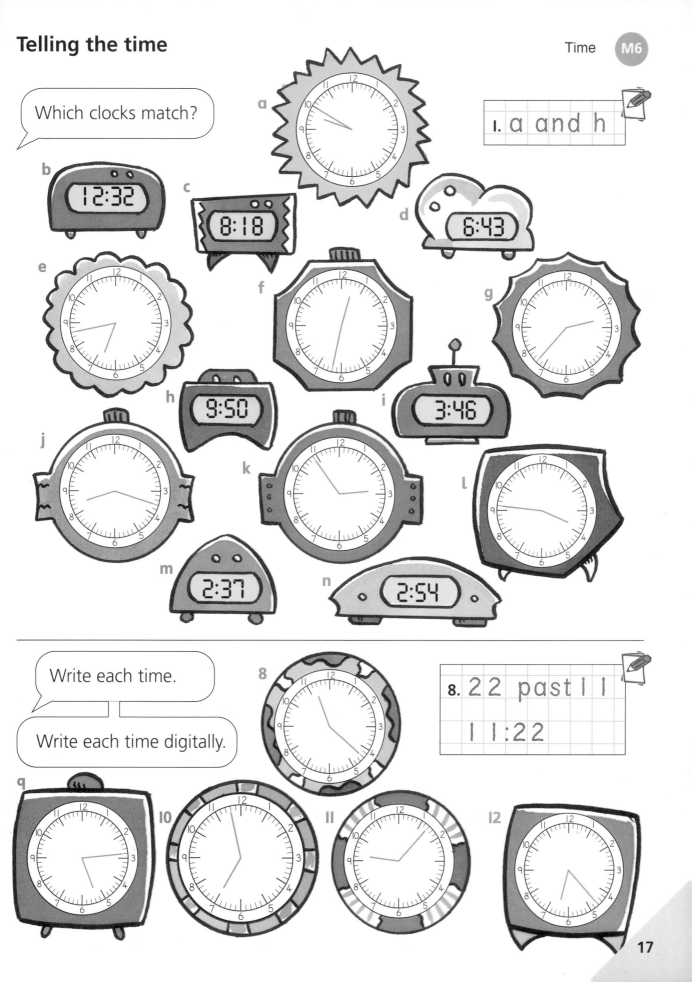

1. a and h

b 12:32

c 8:18

d 6:43

h 9:50

i 3:46

m 2:37

n 2:54

Write each time.

Write each time digitally.

8. 22 past 11

11:22

Telling the time

Write the time shown on each clock.

1. 10:50

1. | 1 | 0 | to | 1 | 1 |

2. 11:08
3. 3:46
4. 1:33
5. 1:55
6. 3:40
7. 5:34
8. 11:48
9. 6:15
10. 8:29
11. 1:18
12. 6:28
13. 12:36
14. 9:38
15. 7:53
16. 10:44
17. 2:27

Write the digital times to match these.

18. 20 to 6

18. 5:40

19. quarter to 9

20. 5 to 2

21. 10 to 10

22. 5 to 11

23. 25 to 8

24. 23 to 9

Explore

Find pairs of numbers that add up to 60.

How many can you find?

23 + 37
28 + 32
29 + 31

Timing

Write the length of each programme.

1 DAILY News
| start | 12:05 |
| end | 12:30 |

1. 25 minutes

2 RAB + ROB
| start | 1:45 |
| end | 2:15 |

3 SPACE COPS
| start | 7:30 |
| end | 9:10 |

4 COWBOY JOE
| start | 12:30 |
| end | 1:10 |

5 CRIME BUSTERS
| start | 4:55 |
| end | 6:15 |

6 FOOTBALL EXTRA!
| start | 6:50 |
| end | 7:25 |

7 WHIZZ KID
| start | 8:50 |
| end | 9:25 |

8 TOP TEN HITS
| start | 3:15 |
| end | 4:10 |

9 ROBO DOG
| start | 2:10 |
| end | 2:45 |

10 STUMPY + POD
| start | 9:05 |
| end | 10:00 |

List the programmes that are 30 minutes long.

| 7:30 | Breakfast TV |
| 8:00 | Cook fast |

| 8:00 | Animal watch |
| 9:30 | News |

| 1:05 | House of fun |
| 1:45 | Dragon Quest |

| 8:55 | Pop charts |
| 9:25 | Redland Road |

| 3:45 | Cartoon time |
| 4:10 | Weather |

| 9:50 | Sports Quiz |
| 10:20 | Film |

| 1:55 | School Daze |
| 2:35 | Go! TV |

Timing

Write each child's race time.

1 Sam
start 4:15
finish 4:37

1. Sam: 2 2 minutes

2 Ann
start 4:20
finish 4:40

3 Jo
start 4:22
finish 4:49

4 Dave
start 4:27
finish 4:51

5 Pindar
start 4:31
finish 4:55

6 Hani
start 4:33
finish 5:01

7 Bill
start 4:38
finish 5:04

8 Zoe
start 4:41
finish 5:09

9 Maya
start 4:45
finish 5:13

10 Sean
start 4:50
finish 5:21

Write the times in order. — Who was quickest? — Who was slowest?

Each child swims for 25 minutes. — Write the times they finish.

11. Ben: 1 0 : 3 5

11 Ben
start 10:10

12 Amit
start 9:08

13 Sue
start 9:25

14 Jade
start 10:17

15 Rob
start 8:33

16 Pat
start 8:48

Timing

Each helicopter ride lasts 55 minutes.

Write the times they finish.

I. 1 : 2 5

1

start 12:30

2

start 2:20

3

start 4:10

4

start 1:05

5

start 10:50

6

start 6:25

7

start 11:55

8

start 3:40

q

start 6:12

Write the finish times if each ride lasts 35 minutes.

Ia. 1 : 0 5

 **Explore**

Use a television schedule. Choose a channel.

Explore the lengths of the programmes during one evening.

Write them in order.

Which programme is longest?

Which is shortest?

24 hour clock

Time M8

Write these as 24 hour clock times.

1 4:30 p.m.

1. 4:30 p.m. → 16:30

2 8:00 a.m.

3 1:15 p.m.

4 3:30 p.m.
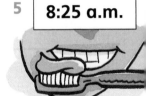

5 8:25 a.m.

6 9:25 p.m.

7 9:00 a.m.

SCHOOL

8 7:20 p.m.

9 7:30 a.m.

10 10:35 a.m.

11 3:00 a.m.

12 5:50 p.m.

13 11:40 a.m.

Write each time as a.m. or p.m.

14

16:50

14. 16:50 → 4:50 p.m.

15

9:45

16

13:02

17

15:21

18

22:48

19

19:21

20

8:48

21

17:53

22

10:08

Space Port	11:40	Asteroid Adventure	16:35
Rocket Launch-pad	12:30	Venus Video	17:05
Mars Café	13:20	The Black Hole	18:10
Pluto Planetarium	14:25	Planetary Fly-by	19:05
Mercury Hyperdrive	15:50	Homeward Bound	20:15

> Write these start times as a.m. or p.m.

1   Mars Café   1. 13:20 → 1:20 p.m.

2   The Black Hole   3   Space Port   4   Homeward Bound

5   Pluto Planetarium   6   Rocket Launch-pad   7   Venus Video

---

> How long is spent at:

8   Asteroid Adventure?   8. 16:35 → 17:05
     30 minutes

9   Space Port?   10   Mars Café?   11   Venus Video?

12   Mercury Hyperdrive?   13   The Black Hole?   14   Planetary Fly-by?

Explore

Design your own Theme Park timetable, using 24 hour clock times.

Each hockey match lasts 25 minutes.

Write the finish times.

1. | 1 | 4 | : | 0 | 0 |

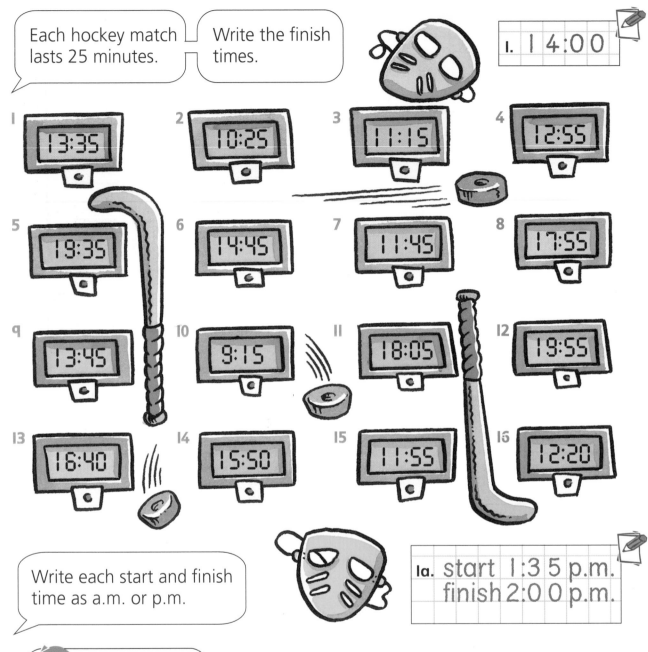

1. 13:35
2. 10:25
3. 11:15
4. 12:55
5. 19:35
6. 14:45
7. 11:45
8. 17:55
9. 13:45
10. 9:15
11. 18:05
12. 19:55
13. 16:40
14. 15:50
15. 11:55
16. 12:20

Write each start and finish time as a.m. or p.m.

1a. start 1:35 p.m.
    finish 2:00 p.m.

Explore

Write the timetable for a hockey tournament.

The first match must start at 14:00.

Each game is 25 minutes long.

Allow 10 minutes between each game.

Write the start and finish times for 10 games.

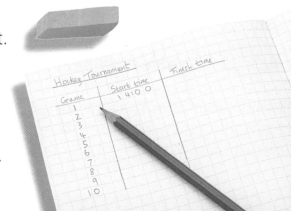

Copy each shape.

Draw the:
horizontal lines in red,
vertical lines in blue,
other lines in green.

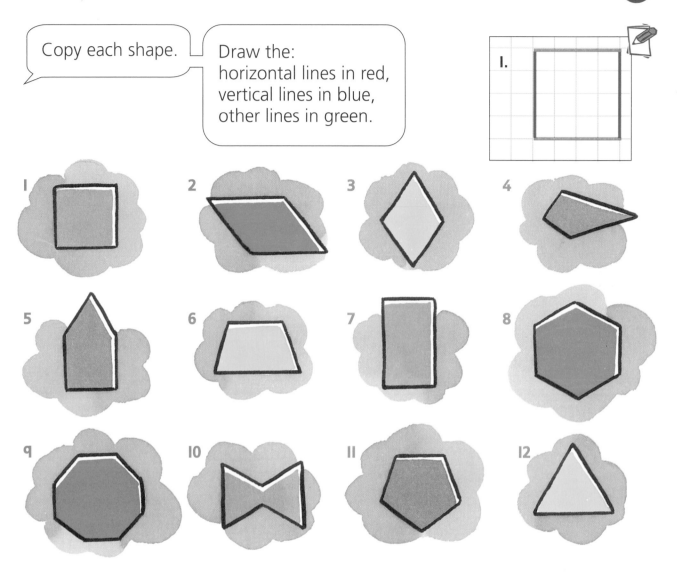

1.

1

2

3

4

5

6

7

8

9

10

11

12

Explore

Here are 2 rectangular grids.

Count how many horizontal and vertical lines you need to draw each grid.

Explore for different grids.

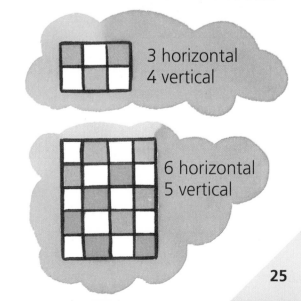

3 horizontal
4 vertical

6 horizontal
5 vertical

Parallel lines

Are these lines parallel?

1

1. yes

2

3

4

5

Do these pictures show parallel lines?

6

6. no

7

8

9

10

11

12

13

14

Copy this plan of a football pitch.

Colour sets of parallel lines.

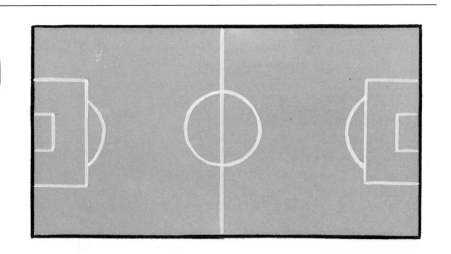

Parallel and perpendicular lines

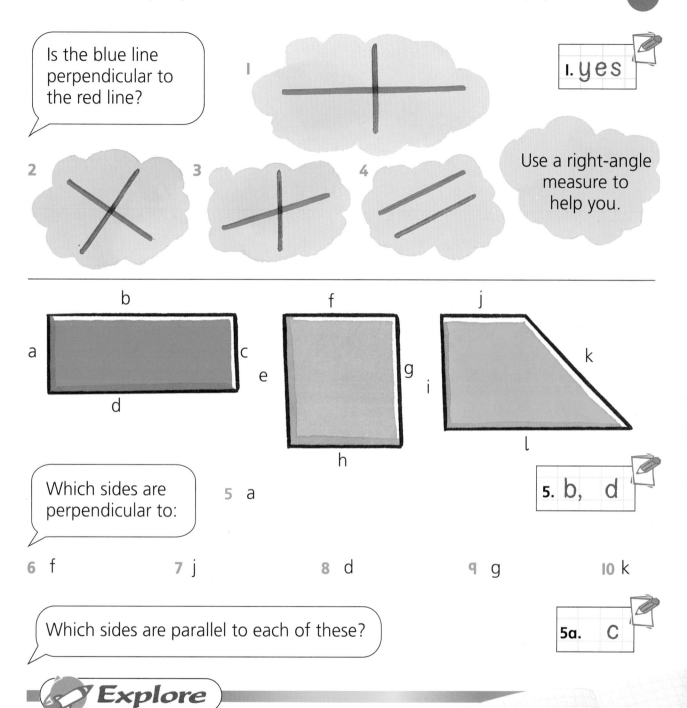

Is the blue line perpendicular to the red line?

Use a right-angle measure to help you.

1. yes

Which sides are perpendicular to:

5 a

5. b, d

6 f   7 j   8 d   9 g   10 k

Which sides are parallel to each of these?

5a. c

Explore

Z has parallel lines.

L has perpendicular lines.

H has parallel and perpendicular lines.

Explore parallel and perpendicular lines in other capital letters.

A   no parallel
     no perpendicular
B
C

Naming shapes

square   rectangle   triangle   pentagon   hexagon

octagon   parallelogram   rhombus   circle

> Write the name of each shape.

1

1. triangle

2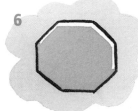

3

4

5

6

7

8

9

10

11

12

13

Explore

Draw a triangle and cut it out.

Draw around it to make a matching triangle and cut this out.

Join the 2 triangles to make a parallelogram.

Explore for different shaped triangles.

Naming shapes

Are these parallelograms?

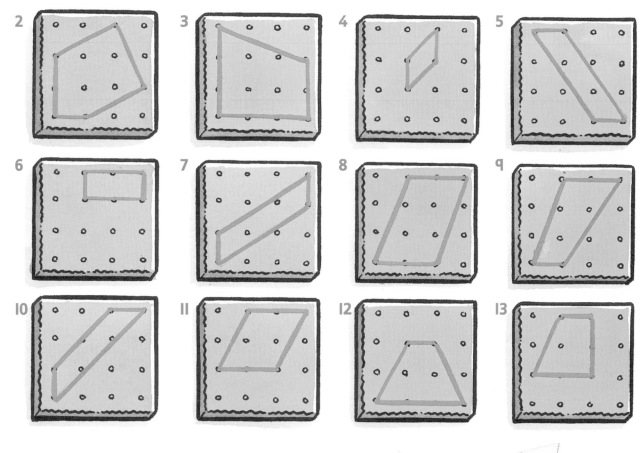

1. yes

Explore

Use isometric paper.

Draw 5 different parallelograms and 5 different rhombuses.

Circles

Measure the radius of each circle.

Double it.

1. r = 1 cm
   double r = 2 cm

A ruler

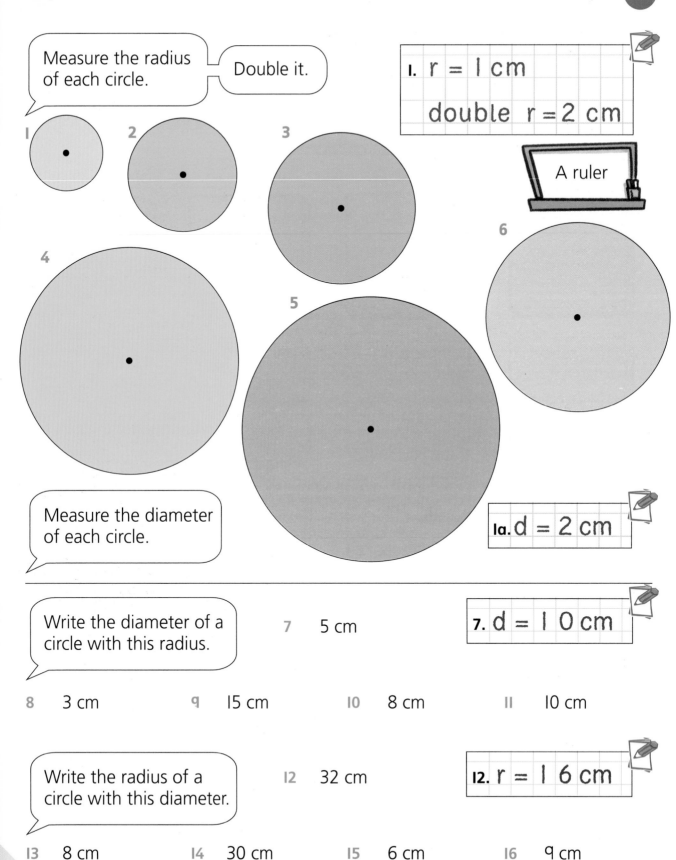

Measure the diameter of each circle.

1a. d = 2 cm

Write the diameter of a circle with this radius.

7   5 cm

7. d = 1 0 cm

8   3 cm   9   15 cm   10   8 cm   11   10 cm

Write the radius of a circle with this diameter.

12   32 cm

12. r = 1 6 cm

13   8 cm   14   30 cm   15   6 cm   16   9 cm

30

Circles

> Find each of these.

> Measure the diameter and circumference.

I.	d = 2·5 cm
	c = 7·5 cm

1

2

3

> Use a ruler and damp cotton.

> Measure the diameter of each badge.

> Use the diameter to find the approximate circumference.

4.	d = 4 cm
	c = 12 cm

4

5

6

7

8

q

> Use damp cotton to check one circumference.

Measure the radius of each circle.

Use the radius to find the approximate circumference.

red: r = 1 cm

c = 6 cm

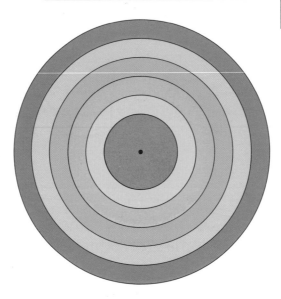

Find the approximate diameter of each of these.

1. d = 3 0 cm

1. c = 90 cm

2. c = 120 cm

3. c = 9 cm

4. c = 36 cm

5. c = 150 cm

6. c = 3 cm

7. c = 60 cm

8. c = 6 cm

9. c = 24 cm

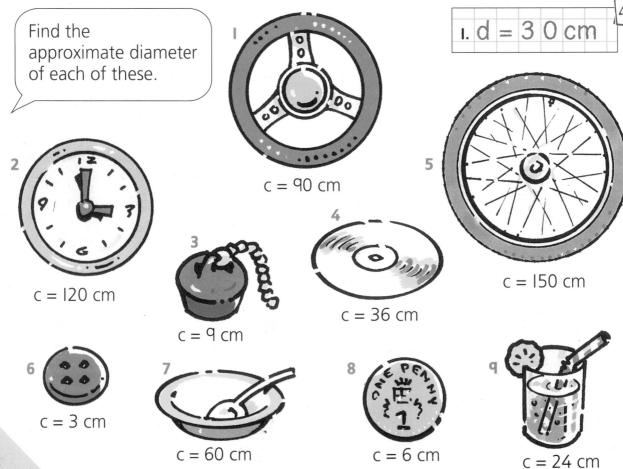

Naming shapes

cone   pyramid   sphere   prism

cube   cuboid   cylinder

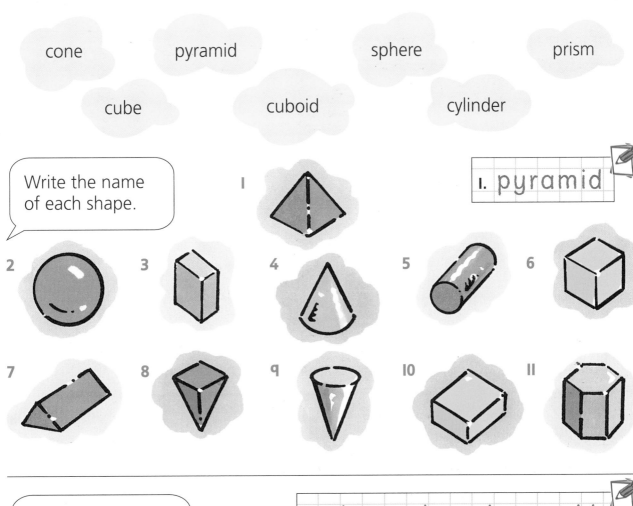

Write the name of each shape.

1

2

3

4

5

6

7

8

9

10

11

1. pyramid

Which types of pyramid are these?

12. triangle-based pyramid

12   13   14   15

Which types of prism are these?

16. pentagonal prism

16   17   18   19

Which shapes have these nets?

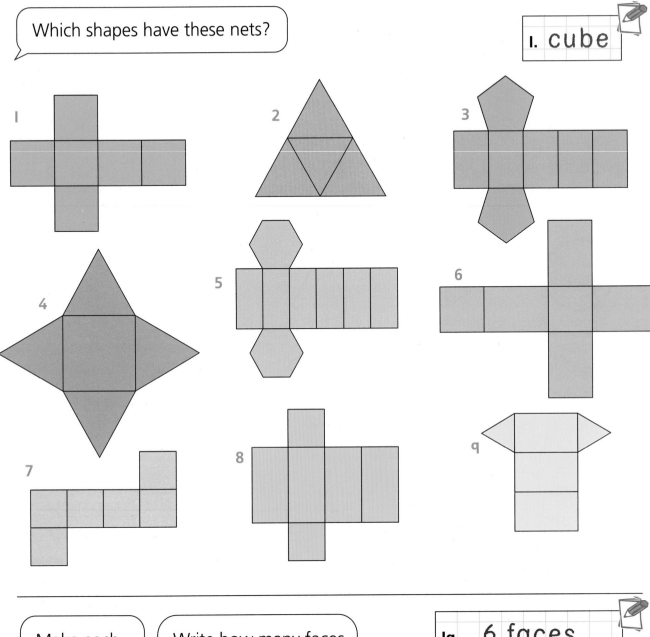

I. cube

la. 6 faces
    12 edges
    8 vertices

Make each shape.

Write how many faces, edges and vertices.

Describe the faces of each shape.

lb. cube: 6 squares

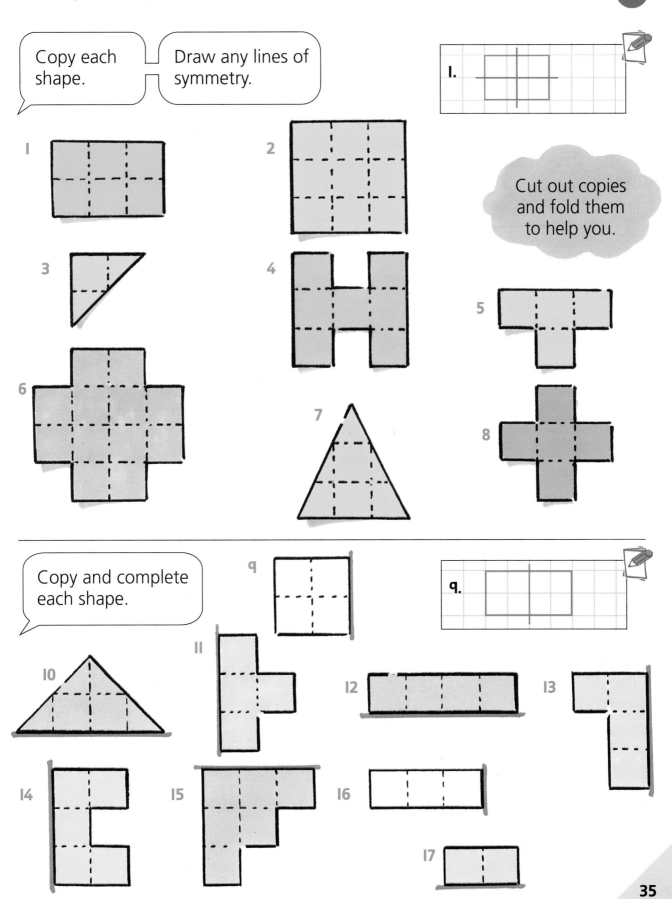

Copy each shape. Draw any lines of symmetry.

I.

1

2

Cut out copies and fold them to help you.

3

4

5

6

7

8

Copy and complete each shape.

9

q.

10

11

12

13

14

15

16

17

Line symmetry

Copy each pattern. Draw any lines of symmetry.

I.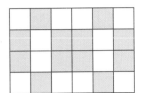

1

2

3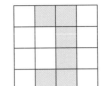

4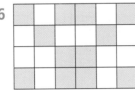

5

6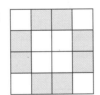

7

8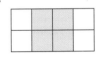

9

10

11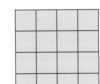

12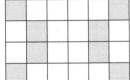

Explore

Make 4 square tiles like this:

Arrange them to make a large square.

Investigate different patterns.

Record in your book any patterns that have symmetry.

Line symmetry

Copy each shape.

Draw any lines of symmetry.

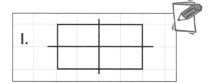

I.

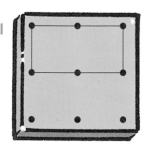 1

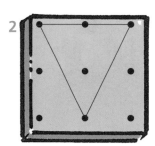 2

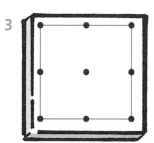 3

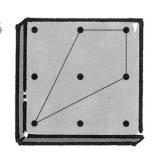 4

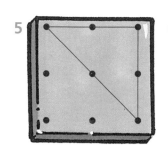 5

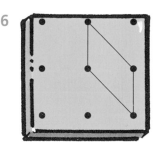 6

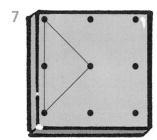 7

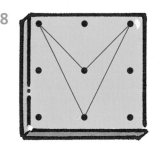 8

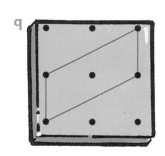 9

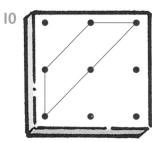 10

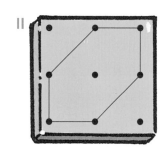 11

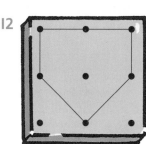 12

A B C D E F G H I J K L M
N O P Q R S T U V W X Y Z

Do these letters have lines of symmetry?

Copy and draw any lines of symmetry.

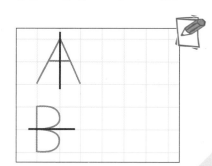

Rotational symmetry

Do these pictures have rotational symmetry?

1

I. yes

2

3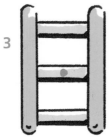

4

5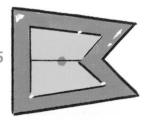

6

7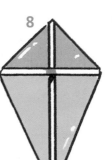

8

q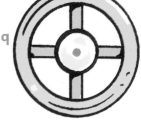

Write how many times each shape matches itself in one complete turn.

Ia. 5

Do these pictures have rotational symmetry?

10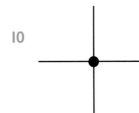

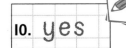
10. yes

11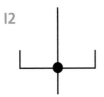

12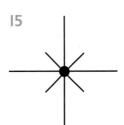

13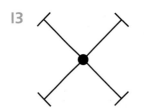

14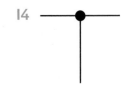

15

Write how many times each shape matches itself in one complete turn.

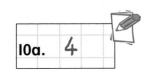
10a. 4

Rotational symmetry

Draw the position of each shape after each of 4 quarter turns.

1.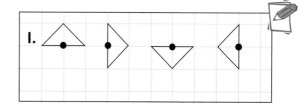

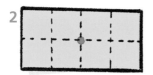

2

3

4

5

6

7

8

9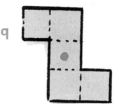

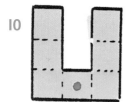  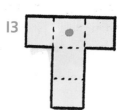

10

11

12

13

Does each shape have rotational symmetry?

1. no

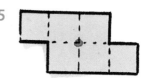 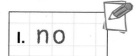

Explore

Check that these patterns have rotational symmetry.

Draw some more patterns on a 3 × 3 grid.

How many can you draw that have rotational symmetry?

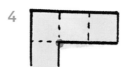

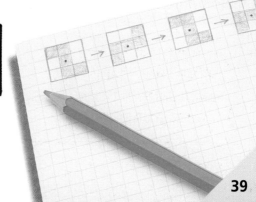

These shapes have rotational symmetry.

Write how many times each shape matches itself in one complete turn.

1. 4

1

2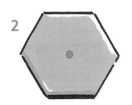

3

4

5

6

7

8

9

10

11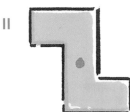

12

Do these patterns have rotational symmetry?

13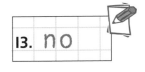

13. no

14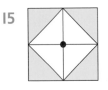

15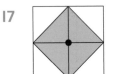

16

17

18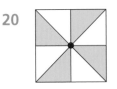

19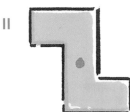

20

Write how many times each pattern matches itself in one complete turn.

21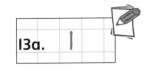

13a. 1

40

Tessellating

Look at these patterns.

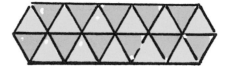

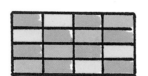

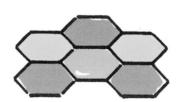
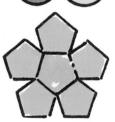

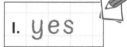

Do these shapes tessellate?

1. yes

2 3 4 5

6 3  7 8 9 10

Explore

Choose one of the tessellating shapes from above.

Trace it and cut out several copies.

Stick the shapes to make a tessellating pattern.

Tessellating

Draw this shape on squared paper.

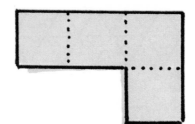

Cut out 8 copies.

Join them to make these tessellating patterns.

Draw each pattern.

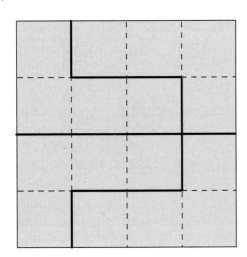

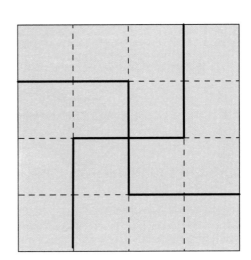

Make your own tessellating patterns using these shapes.

Draw each pattern.

Explore

Cut a rectangle from squared paper.

Cut out a triangle from one side, and stick it on the opposite side.

Make several copies of the new shape.

Test them to see if they tessellate.

Write how many right-angles.

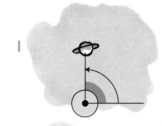

1. I right-angle

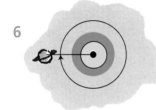 2

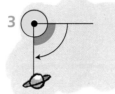 3

4

5

6

7

8

9

Write how many degrees in each turn.

1a. 9 0°

Write how many right-angles clockwise from:

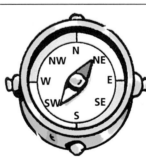

10. 2 right-angles

10	N to S	11	E to N	12	W to N	13	N to NE

14	SW to NE	15	NW to E	16	NE to NW	17	SE to W

18	S to W	19	SW to W	20	SE to SW	21	N to SE

Write how many degrees in each turn.

10a. I 8 0°

Degrees

Write how many right-angles turned by the minute hand.

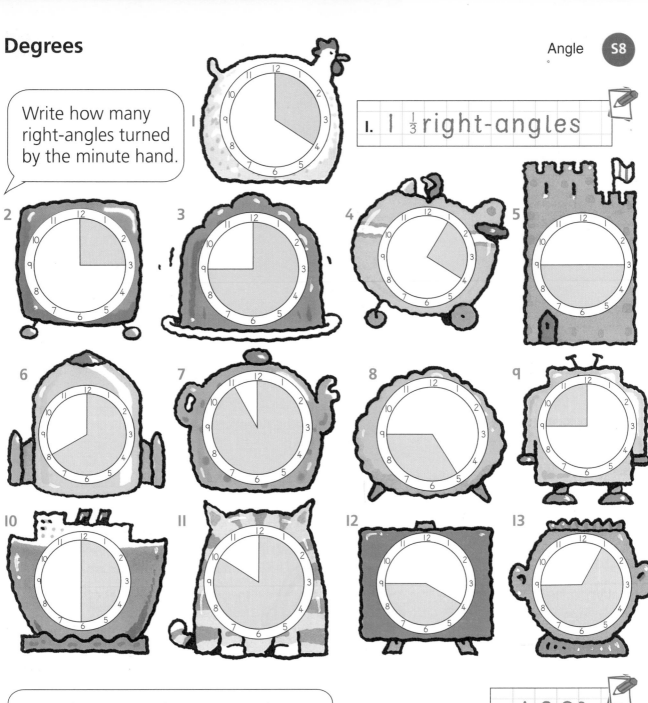

1. $1\frac{1}{3}$ right-angles

Write how many degrees in each turn.

1a. 120°

Write how many degrees turned by the minute hand in:

14	5 minutes

14. 30°

15	30 minutes	16	15 minutes	17	50 minutes	18	25 minutes
19	40 minutes	20	60 minutes	21	35 minutes	22	10 minutes

Degrees

 60° **a**

135° **b**

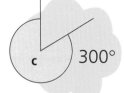 **c** 300°

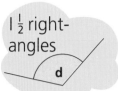 $1\frac{1}{2}$ right-angles **d**

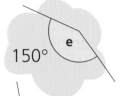 150° **e**

1 right-angle **f**

30° **g**

h $\frac{1}{2}$ right angle

i $2\frac{1}{2}$ right-angles

$\frac{1}{3}$ right angle **j**

k 2 right-angles

l 90°

Which of these angles are:

1 less than 90°?

1. a, g, h, j

2 between 90° and 180°?

3 the same?

4 more than 90°?

By how many degrees is:

5 **c** larger than **a**

5. 240°

6 **d** larger than **g**

7 **f** smaller than **k**

8 **h** smaller than **e**

9 **k** larger than **b**

10 **a** larger than **g**

11 **b** smaller than **e**

Write all the angles in order, from smallest to largest.

30°, 45°,

Measuring angles

Write how many degrees in each angle.

1. 60°

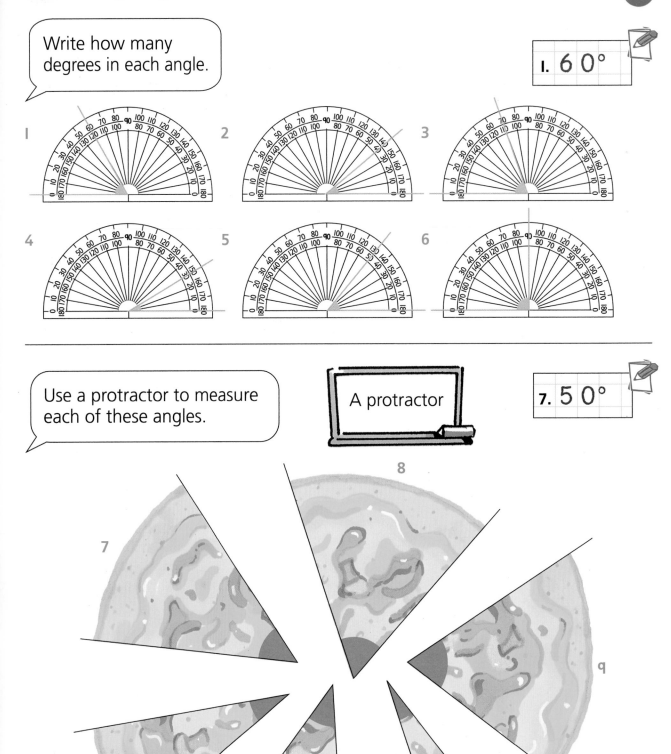

Use a protractor to measure each of these angles.

A protractor

7. 50°

Measuring angles

Estimate, then measure each angle.

A protractor

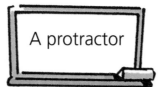

1. estimate: 38°
measure: 40°

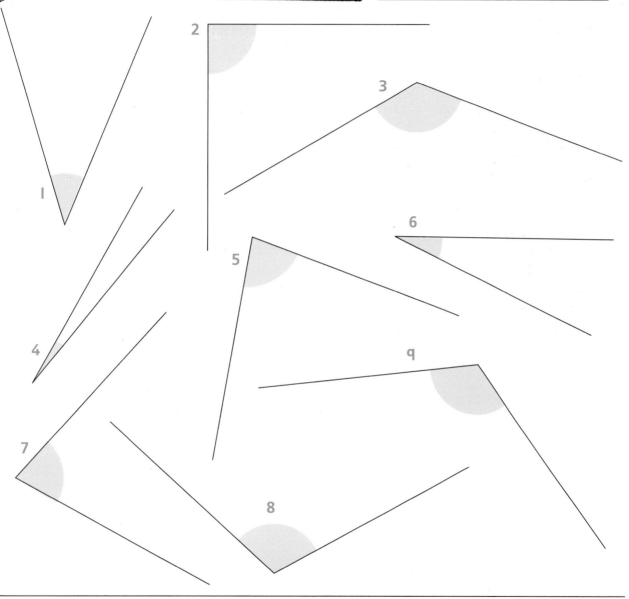

1

2

3

6

5

4

q

7

8

Draw each of these angles, by estimating.

Measure each with a protractor to check.

A ruler
A protractor

| 10 | 50° | 11 | 90° | 12 | 20° | 13 | 70° |
| 14 | 120° | 15 | 45° | 16 | 180° | 17 | 135° |

Measuring angles

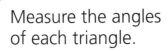

Measure the angles of each triangle.

A protractor

a. 90°

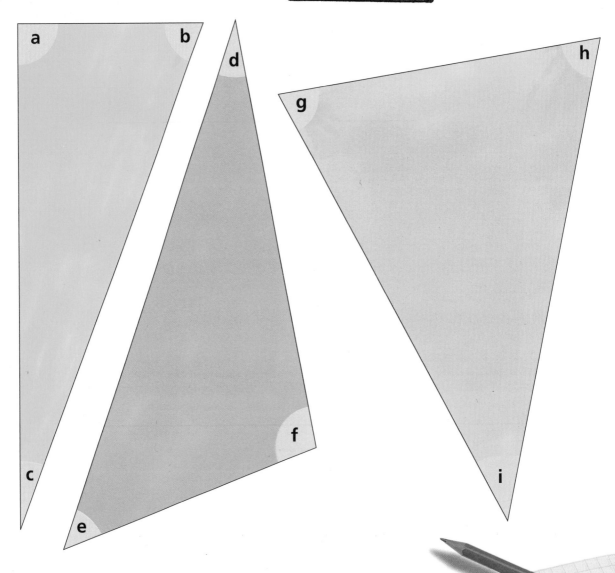

Draw 5 large triangles.

Measure the angles of each.

Explore the totals of the angles of each triangle.

Coordinates

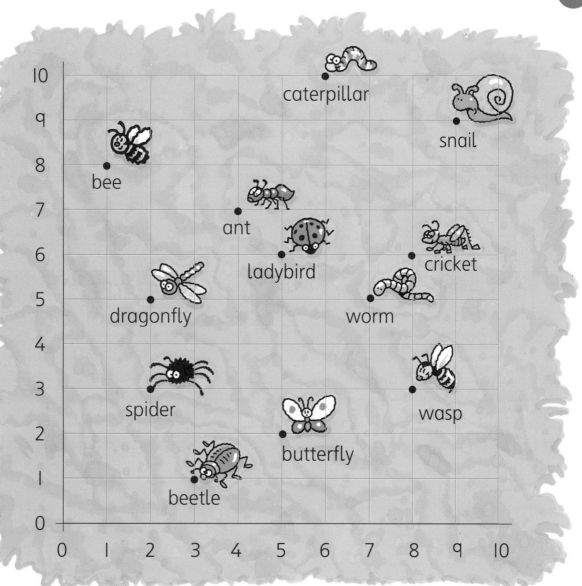

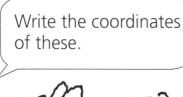

Write the coordinates of these.

spider

1. spider: (2,3)

2
wasp

3
cricket

4
snail

5
ant

6
beetle

Write what is at these coordinates.

7 (1,8)

7. bee

8 (5,6)   **9** (2,5)   **10** (5,2)   **11** (7,5)   **12** (6,10)

49

Coordinates

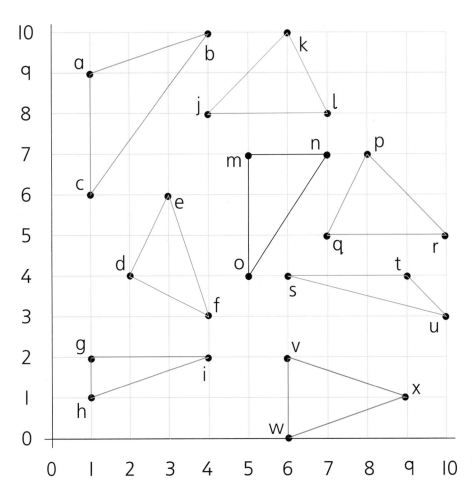

Write the coordinates of each triangle's corners.

a. (1,9)

Draw a 10 × 10 grid. | Plot these sets of coordinates. | Join them to make shapes.

1
(2,4)   (4,4)
(4,6)   (2,6)

2
(5,7)   (7,8)
(6,5)

3
(2,1)   (2,3)
(5,1)   (5,3)

4
(7,1)   (9,2)
(7,3)   (9,3)

5
(1,10)   (3,10)
(1,8)   (4,8)

6
(8,10)   (10,10)
(9,5)

50

Coordinates

Draw a 10 × 10 grid.	Plot these points.	Join them in order to find a picture.

1	(3,1)	2	(4,2)	3	(4,4)	4	(0,4)	5	(1,5)
6	(4,6)	7	(4,8)	8	(5,9)	9	(6,8)	10	(6,6)
11	(9,5)	12	(10,4)	13	(6,4)	14	(6,2)	15	(7,1)

Write the coordinates of each point in the picture.

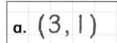

a. (3, 1)

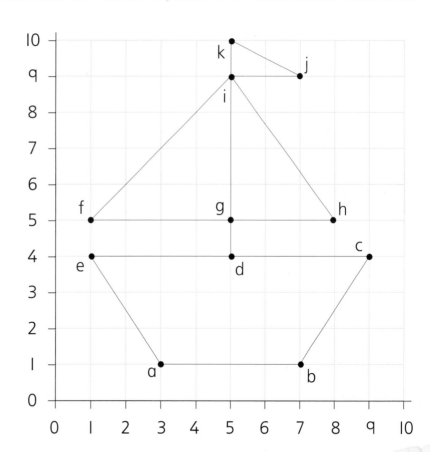

Explore

Write pairs of coordinates that add to make 10: (0,10), (1,9), (2,8).

Plot them on a 10 × 10 grid. What do you notice?

Try for pairs that add to make 7, 11, 14 …

Bar-line graphs

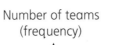

30 teams played one game of football each on Saturday.

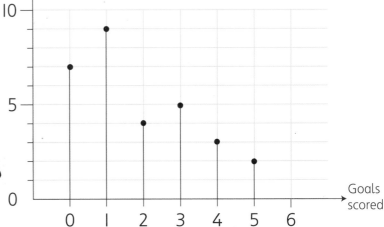

Number of teams (frequency)

Goals scored by 30 teams on Saturday

Goals scored

How many teams scored exactly:

| 3 goals?

1. 5

2 0 goals?
3 5 goals?
4 1 goal?

5 2 goals?
6 4 goals?
7 6 goals?

How many goals were scored:

8 most often?

8. 1

9 5 times?
10 7 times?
11 3 times?

12 4 times?
13 2 times?
14 more than 5 times?

How many teams scored:

15 more than 3 goals?

15. 5

16 less than 2 goals?
17 1 or 2 goals?
18 an odd number of goals?
19 at least 3 goals?

Bar-line graphs

Copy and complete the bar-line graph to show the dates of these 40 annuals.

How many annuals are from:

1. 6

Dates of 40 annuals

Number of annuals (frequency)

20

10

0

90 91 92 93 94 95 96 97
Year

1   1993?

2   1990?   3   1995?   4   1997?   5   1994?   6   1996?

Explore

Deal 26 cards from a shuffled pack.

Draw a bar-line graph to show how many there are of each suit.

Bar-line graphs

Here are 32 dice throws.

Draw a bar-line graph to show the results.

How many dice throws showed:

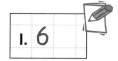

1. 6

 1   2   3   4   5   6

How many throws were:

7   more than 3?

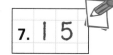

7. 15

8   less than 5?   9   odd?   10   even?

Copy and complete this bar-line graph using the above dice throws.

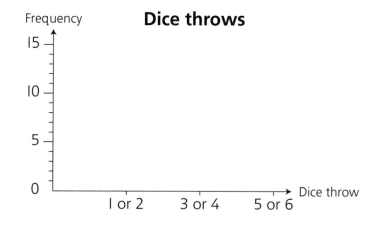

Dice throws

54

Averages

> Write the average distance walked.

I. total: $5 + 3 = 8$ km
average: $8 \div 2 = 4$ km

1
Saturday 5 km

Sunday 3 km

2
Saturday 4 km

Sunday 8 km

3
Saturday 6 km

Sunday 4 km

4
Saturday 7 km

Sunday 7 km

5
Saturday 3 km

Sunday 9 km

6
Saturday 2 km

Sunday 6 km

> Write the average amount of spending money.

7. total: $8 + 5 + 5 = 18$ p
average: $18 \div 3 = 6$ p

7
8p 5p 5p

8
10p 13p 7p

9
12p 9p 6p

10
13p 9p 11p

11
8p 7p 6p

12
5p 7p 3p

13
12p 15p 18p

14
4p 3p 2p

15
5p 3p 4p

Averages

Write the average scores.

1. total: $4 + 8 = 12$
average: $12 \div 3 = 4$

1 | 4 | 8 | 0 |

2 | 10 | 4 |

3 | 8 | 10 | 3 |

4 | 6 | 14 | 7 |

5 | 12 | 8 |

6 | 12 | 5 | 1 |

7 | 15 | 7 |

8 | 4 | 18 | 8 |

Write the average times.

9. total: $3 + 5 = 8$ minutes
average: $8 \div 2 = 4$ minutes

9
3 minutes
5 minutes

10
5 minutes
6 minutes
4 minutes
5 minutes

11
6 minutes
5 minutes
4 minutes

12
12 minutes
14 minutes

13
6 minutes
5 minutes
8 minutes
9 minutes

14
5 minutes
7 minutes
9 minutes

15
8 minutes
6 minutes

16
8 minutes
11 minutes
9 minutes
12 minutes

Averages

Write the average scores.

1. total: $3 + 5 = 8$
average: $8 \div 2 = 4$

2

3

4

5

6

7

8

9

10

Explore

These cards have an average score of 6.
Write 3 other pairs that have an average
score of 6.

Write sets of 3 cards, 4 cards, 5 cards …
that have an average score of 6.

Ladles and jellyspoons:
I come before you
To stand behind you
And tell you something
I know nothing about.

Next Thursday,
The day after Friday,
There'll be a ladies'
meeting
For men only.

Wear your best clothes
If you haven't any,
And if you come
Please stay at home.

Admission is free,
You can pay on the door.
We'll give you a seat
So you can sit on the
floor.

It makes no difference
Where you sit;
The kid in the gallery
Is sure to spit.

Copy and complete the table to show the lengths of the words in the poem.

Word length	Frequency
1–3	
4–6	
7–9	
10+	

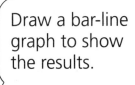

Draw a bar-line graph to show the results.

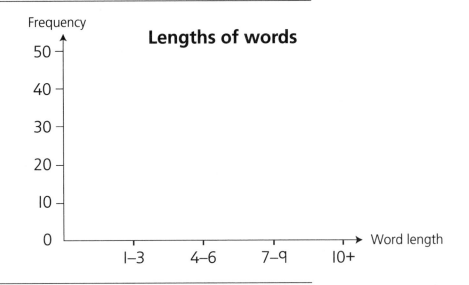

Lengths of words

How many words had:

1 1–3 letters?

2 7–9 letters?

3 4–6 letters?

4 more than 6 letters?

5 less than 7 letters?

Grouped frequency tables

Scores in a game of cards

	Sam		Ali		Jo	
Round 1		16		8		16
Round 2		22		3		30
Round 3		29		30		29
Round 4		11		17		8
Round 5		8		15		20
Round 6		12		27		8
Round 7		16		30		6
Round 8		7		5		17
Round 9		12		11		11

Put the scores in groups and draw a frequency table.

Score	Frequency
1-5	2
6-10	
11-15	

Draw a bar-line graph to show the results.

Explore

Remove the picture cards and jokers from a pack of cards.

Make sets of 3 cards. Add the values to find a score for each set.

Draw a frequency table to show the results.

59

Grouped frequency tables

Spelling scores

Copy and complete the table to show the scores in the spelling test.

Draw a bar-line graph to show the results.

Score	Frequency
10–12	
13–15	
16–18	
19–21	
22–24	

 **Explore**

Find 20 library books.

Find how many pages in each.

Complete a grouped frequency table, then a bar-line graph to show the results.

Listing outcomes

 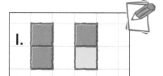

 Use 2 colours: red and yellow.

Draw 4 different strips, each 2 squares long.

1.

Use 3 colours: red, blue and yellow.

Draw as many strips as you can, each 2 squares long.

2.
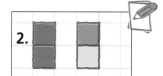

Use 2 colours: yellow and blue.

Draw as many strips as you can, each 3 squares long.

3.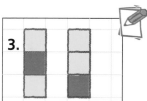

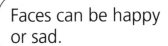
Faces can be happy or sad.

They can wear a hat or not wear a hat.

They can wear a tie or not wear a tie.

Draw 8 different faces using these rules.

 **Explore**

Suppose you are making sandwiches.

For the bread you can choose brown or white.

For the filling you can choose either cheese, chicken or egg.

How many different sandwiches can you make?

egg sandwich on brown bread

Throwing dice

From 24 dice throws, how many do you estimate will be:

1

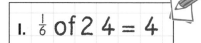

1. $\frac{1}{6}$ of 2 4 = 4

2   3   4   5

Throw a dice 24 times and draw a tally chart to show how many times you throw each number.

Compare the results with your estimates.

Dice throw	Tallies	Total
1		
2		
3		

How many times do you estimate a dice will show 🎲 if it is thrown.

6   30 times?

6. $\frac{1}{6}$ of 3 0 = 5

7   60 times?   8   18 times?   9   36 times?   10   120 times?

From 18 dice throws, how many do you estimate will be:

11   even?

12   odd?

11. $\frac{1}{2}$ of 1 8 = 9

Throw a dice 18 times and draw a tally chart to show how many throws were even or odd.

Compare the results with your estimates.

Dice throw	Tallies	Total
even		
odd		

How many times do you estimate a dice will be even if it is thrown:

13   12 times?

13. $\frac{1}{2}$ of 1 2 = 6

14   24 times?   15   50 times?   16   44 times?   17   110 times?

Picking cubes

> Put 2 yellow, 2 green, I blue and I red cube in a bag.

> If a cube is taken out and put back 24 times how many cubes do you estimate will be:

1. $\frac{1}{6}$ of 2 4 = 4

1	red?	2	green?	3	blue?	4	yellow?

> Take out and put back a cube 24 times, and draw a tally chart to show the colours of the cubes.

> Compare the results with your estimates.

Cube	Tallies	Total
yellow		
green		
blue		
red		

> How many times do you estimate the cube will be yellow if it is taken out and put back:

5. 18 times?

5. $\frac{2}{6}$ of 1 8 = 6

6	42 times?	7	90 times?	8	30 times?	9	36 times?

 Explore

Put 6 coloured cubes in a bag.

If a cube is taken out and put back 24 times, how many do you estimate will be of each colour?

Take out a cube and put it back 24 times, and draw a tally chart to show the colours of the cubes.